Manfred

Manfred
by Lord Byron

Start Publishing PD LLC
Copyright © 2024 by Start Publishing PD LLC

All rights reserved, including the right to reproduce this book or portions thereof in any form whatsoever.

Start Publishing PD is a registered trademark of Start Publishing PD LLC
Manufactured in the United States of America

Cover art: Shutterstock/Taisiya Kozorez

Cover design: Jennifer Do

10 9 8 7 6 5 4 3 2 1

ISBN 979-8-8809-0775-5

Byron undertook "Manfred," his most Gothic work, in late 1816, a few months after the famed ghost-story sessions which provided the initial impetus for Mary Shelley's Frankenstein and John Polidori's The Vampyre, which some argue is based on Byron's fragment of a novel, his brief response to the challenge of the ghost-story sessions. Byron also heard Goethe's Faust about this time, and "Manfred" may also owe something to Matthew Lewis, author of The Monk, who visited Byron a month or two before "Manfred" was begun. The poem was completed in April of 1817 and published in June of that year.

MANFRED A DRAMATIC POEM

'There are more things in heaven and earth, Horatio, Than are dreamt of in your philosophy.'

DRAMATIS PERSONAE

MANFRED
CHAMOIS HUNTER
ABBOT OF ST. MAURICE
MANUEL
HERMAN
WITCH OF THE ALPS
ARIMANES
NEMESIS
THE DESTINIES
SPIRITS, etc

The scene of the Drama is amongst the Higher Alps—partly in the Castle of Manfred, and partly in the Mountains.

ACT I
SCENE I

MANFRED alone.—Scene, a Gothic Gallery.—Time, Midnight.

MANFRED. The lamp must be replenish'd, but even then
It will not burn so long as I must watch.
My slumbers—if I slumber—are not sleep,
But a continuance of enduring thought,
Which then I can resist not: in my heart
There is a vigil, and these eyes but close
To look within; and yet I live, and bear
The aspect and the form of breathing men.
But grief should be the instructor of the wise;
Sorrow is knowledge: they who know the most   10
Must mourn the deepest o'er the fatal truth,
The Tree of Knowledge is not that of Life.
Philosophy and science, and the springs
Of wonder, and the wisdom of the world,
I have essay'd, and in my mind there is
A power to make these subject to itself—
But they avail not: I have done men good,
And I have met with good even among men—
But this avail'd not: I have had my foes,
And none have baffled, many fallen before me—   20
But this avail'd not: Good, or evil, life,
Powers, passions, all I see in other beings,
Have been to me as rain unto the sands,
Since that all-nameless hour. I have no dread,
And feel the curse to have no natural fear
Nor fluttering throb, that beats with hopes or wishes
Or lurking love of something on the earth.

Now to my task.—
        Mysterious Agency!
Ye spirits of the unbounded Universe,
Whom I have sought in darkness and in light!   30
Ye, who do compass earth about, and dwell
In subtler essence! ye, to whom the tops
Of mountains inaccessible are haunts,
And earth's and ocean's caves familiar things—
I call upon ye by the written charm
Which gives me power upon you—Rise! appear! [A pause.
They come not yet.—Now by the voice of him
Who is the first among you; by this sign,
Which makes you tremble; by the claims of him
Who is undying,—Rise! appear!—Appear!   [A pause.   40
If it be so.—Spirits of earth and air,
Ye shall not thus elude me: by a power,
Deeper than all yet urged, a tyrant-spell,
Which had its birthplace in a star condemn'd,
The burning wreck of a demolish'd world,
A wandering hell in the eternal space;
By the strong curse which is upon my soul,
The thought which is within me and around me,
I do compel ye to my will. Appear!

[A star is seen at the darker end of the gallery: it is stationary; and a voice is heard singing.

      FIRST SPIRIT.

  Mortal! to thy bidding bow'd,   50
    From my mansion in the cloud,
  Which the breath of twilight builds,
    And the summer's sunset gilds
  With the azure and vermilion
    Which is mix'd for my pavilion;

Though thy quest may be forbidden,
  On a star-beam I have ridden,
To thine adjuration bow'd;
  Mortal—be thy wish avow'd!

    Voice of the SECOND SPIRIT.

Mont Blanc is the monarch of mountains;   60
  They crown'd him long ago
On a throne of rocks, in a robe of clouds,
  With a diadem of snow.
Around his waist are forests braced,
  The Avalanche in his hand;
But ere it fall, that thundering ball
  Must pause for my command.
The Glacier's cold and restless mass
  Moves onward day by day;
But I am he who bids it pass,   70
  Or with its ice delay.
I am the spirit of the place,
  Could make the mountain bow
And quiver to his cavern'd base—
And what with me wouldst Thou?

    Voice of the THIRD SPIRIT.

In the blue depth of the waters,
  Where the wave hath no strife,
Where the wind is a stranger
  And the sea-snake hath life,
Where the Mermaid is decking   80
  Her green hair with shells;
Like the storm on the surface
  Came the sound of thy spells;
O'er my calm Hall of Coral

The deep echo roll'd—
To the Spirit of Ocean
  Thy wishes unfold!

FOURTH SPIRIT.

Where the slumbering earthquake
  Lies pillow'd on fire,
And the lakes of bitumen   90
  Rise boilingly higher;
Where the roots of the Andes
  Strike deep in the earth,
As their summits to heaven
  Shoot soaringly forth;
I have quitted my birthplace,
  Thy bidding to bide—
Thy spell hath subdued me,
  Thy will be my guide!

FIFTH SPIRIT.

I am the Rider of the wind,   100
  The Stirrer of the storm;
The hurricane I left behind
  Is yet with lightning warm;
To speed to thee, o'er shore and sea
  I swept upon the blast:
The fleet I met sail'd well, and yet
  'T will sink ere night be past.

SIXTH SPIRIT.

My dwelling is the shadow of the night,
  Why doth thy magic torture me with light?

SEVENTH SPIRIT

The star which rules thy destiny 110
  Was ruled, ere earth began, by me:
It was a world as fresh and fair
  As e'er revolved round sun in air;
Its course was free and regular,
  Space bosom'd not a lovelier star.
The hour arrived—and it became
  A wandering mass of shapeless flame,
A pathless comet, and a curse,
  The menace of the universe;
Still rolling on with innate force, 120
  Without a sphere, without a course,
A bright deformity on high,
  The monster of the upper sky!
And thou! beneath its influence born—
  Thou worm! whom I obey and scorn—
Forced by a power (which is not thine,
  And lent thee but to make thee mine)
For this brief moment to descend,
  Where these weak spirits round thee bend
And parley with a thing like thee— 130
  What wouldst thou, Child of Clay! with me?

The SEVEN SPIRITS

Earth, ocean, air, night, mountains, winds, thy star,
  Are at thy beck and bidding, Child of Clay!
Before thee at thy quest their spirits are—
  What wouldst thou with us, son of mortals—say?

MANFRED. Forgetfulness—

FIRST SPIRIT. Of what—of whom—and why?

MANFRED. Of that which is within me; read it there—
Ye know it, and I cannot utter it.

SPIRIT. We can but give thee that which we possess:
Ask of us subjects, sovereignty, the power   140
O'er earth, the whole, or portion, or a sign
Which shall control the elements, whereof
We are the dominators,—each and all,
These shall be thine.

MANFRED. Oblivion, self-oblivion—
Can ye not wring from out the hidden realms
Ye offer so profusely what I ask?

SPIRIT. It is not in our essence, in our skill;
But—thou mayst die.

MANFRED. Will death bestow it on me?

SPIRIT. We are immortal, and do not forget;
We are eternal; and to us the past   150
Is, as the future, present. Art thou answered?

MANFRED. Ye mock me—but the power which brought ye here
Hath made you mine. Slaves, scoff not at my will!
The mind, the spirit, the Promethean spark,
The lightning of my being, is as bright,
Pervading, and far-darting as your own,
And shall not yield to yours, though coop'd in clay!
Answer, or I will teach you what I am.

SPIRIT. We answer as we answer'd; our reply
Is even in thine own words.

MANFRED.   Why say ye so?   160

SPIRIT. If, as thou say'st, thine essence be as ours,
We have replied in telling thee, the thing
Mortals call death hath nought to do with us.

MANFRED. I then have call'd ye from your realms in vain;
Ye cannot, or ye will not, aid me.

SPIRIT. Say;
What we possess we offer; it is thine:
Bethink ere thou dismiss us, ask again—
Kingdom, and sway, and strength, and length of days—

MANFRED. Accursèd! what have I to do with days?
They are too long already.—Hence—begone!   170

SPIRIT. Yet pause: being here, our will would do thee service;
Bethink thee, is there then no other gift
Which we can make not worthless in thine eyes?

MANFRED. No, none: yet stay—one moment, ere we part—
I would behold ye face to face. I hear
Your voices, sweet and melancholy sounds,
As music on the waters; and I see
The steady aspect of a clear large star;
But nothing more. Approach me as ye are,
Or one, or all, in your accustom'd forms.   180

SPIRIT. We have no forms, beyond the elements
Of which we are the mind and principle:
But choose a form—in that we will appear.

MANFRED. I have no choice, there is no form on earth
Hideous or beautiful to me. Let him,
Who is most powerful of ye, take such aspect
As unto him may seem most fitting.—Come!

Seventh spirit (appearing in the shape of a beautiful female figure). Behold!

MANFRED. Oh God! if it be thus, and thou
Art not a madness and a mockery
I yet might be most happy—I will clasp thee,   190
And we again will be—   [The figure vanishes.
        My heart is crushed!
           [MANFRED falls senseless.

(A voice is heard in the Incantation which follows.)

When the moon is on the wave,
  And the glow-worm in the grass,
And the meteor on the grave,
  And the wisp on the morass;
When the falling stars are shooting,
And the answer'd owls are hooting,
And the silent leaves are still
In the shadow of the hill,
Shall my soul be upon thine,   200
With a power and with a sign.

Though thy slumber may be deep,
Yet thy spirit shall not sleep;
There are shades which will not vanish,
There are thoughts thou canst not banish;
By a power to thee unknown,
Thou canst never be alone;
Thou art wrapt as with a shroud,
Thou art gather'd in a cloud;
And forever shalt thou dwell   210
In the spirit of this spell.

Though thou seest me not pass by,

Thou shalt feel me with thine eye
As a thing that, though unseen,
Must be near thee, and hath been;
And when in that secret dread
Thou hast turn'd around thy head,
Thou shalt marvel I am not
As thy shadow on the spot,
And the power which thou dost feel   220
Shall be what thou must conceal.

And a magic voice and verse
Hath baptized thee with a curse;
And a spirit of the air
Hath begirt thee with a snare;
In the wind there is a voice
Shall forbid thee to rejoice;
And to thee shall Night deny
All the quiet of her sky;
And the day shall have a sun,   230
Which shall make thee wish it done.

From thy false tears I did distil
An essence which hath strength to kill;
From thy own heart I then did wring
The black blood in its blackest spring;
From thy own smile I snatch'd the snake,
For there it coil'd as in a brake;
From thy own lip I drew the charm
Which gave all these their chiefest harm;
In proving every poison known,   240
I found the strongest was thine own.
By thy cold breast and serpent smile,
By thy unfathom'd gulfs of guile,
By that most seeming virtuous eye,
By thy shut soul's hypocrisy;

By the perfection of thine art
Which pass'd for human thine own heart;
By thy delight in others' pain,
And by thy brotherhood of Cain,
I call upon thee! and compel   250
Thyself to be thy proper Hell!

And on thy head I pour the vial
Which doth devote thee to this trial;
Nor to slumber, nor to die,
Shall be in thy destiny;
Though thy death shall still seem near
To thy wish, but as a fear;
Lo! the spell now works around thee,
And the clankless chain hath bound thee;
O'er thy heart and brain together   260
Hath the word been pass'd—now wither!

SCENE II

The Mountain of the Jungfrau.—Time, Morning.—

MANFRED alone upon the Cliffs.

MANFRED. The spirits I have raised abandon me,
The spells which I have studied baffled me,
The remedy I reck'd of tortured me;
I lean no more on super-human aid,
It hath no power upon the past, and for
The future, till the past be gulf'd in darkness,
It is not of my search.—My mother Earth!
And thou fresh breaking Day, and you, ye Mountains,
Why are ye beautiful? I cannot love ye.   270
And thou, the bright eye of the universe
That openest over all, and unto all
Art a delight—thou shin'st not on my heart.
And you, ye crags, upon whose extreme edge
I stand, and on the torrent's brink beneath
Behold the tall pines dwindled as to shrubs
In dizziness of distance; when a leap,
A stir, a motion, even a breath, would bring
My breast upon its rocky bosom's bed
To rest forever—wherefore do I pause?   280
I feel the impulse—yet I do not plunge;
I see the peril—yet do not recede;
And my brain reels—and yet my foot is firm.
There is a power upon me which withholds,
And makes it my fatality to live;
If it be life to wear within myself
This barrenness of spirit, and to be

My own soul's sepulchre, for I have ceased
To justify my deeds unto myself—
The last infirmity of evil. Ay,   290
Thou winged and cloud-cleaving minister,   [An eagle passes.
Whose happy flight is highest into heaven,
Well may'st thou swoop so near me—I should be
Thy prey, and gorge thine eaglets; thou art gone
Where the eye cannot follow thee; but thine
Yet pierces downward, onward, or above,
With a pervading vision.—Beautiful!
How beautiful is all this visible world!
How glorious in its action and itself!
But we, who name ourselves its sovereigns, we,   300
Half dust, half deity, alike unfit
To sink or soar, with our mix'd essence make
A conflict of its elements, and breathe
The breath of degradation and of pride,
Contending with low wants and lofty will,
Till our mortality predominates,
And men are what they name not to themselves,
And trust not to each other. Hark! the note,
           [The Shepherd's pipe in the distance is heard.
The natural music of the mountain reed
(For here the patriarchal days are not   310
A pastoral fable) pipes in the liberal air,
Mix'd with the sweet bells of the sauntering herd;
My soul would drink those echoes.—Oh, that I were
The viewless spirit of a lovely sound,
A living voice, a breathing harmony,
A bodiless enjoyment—born and dying
With the blessed tone which made me!

    Enter from below a CHAMOIS HUNTER.

CHAMOIS HUNTER. Even so

This way the chamois leapt: her nimble feet
Have baffled me; my gains to-day will scarce
Repay my break-neck travail.—What is here?   320
Who seems not of my trade, and yet hath reach'd
A height which none even of our mountaineers
Save our best hunters, may attain: his garb
Is goodly, his mien manly, and his air
Proud as a freeborn peasant's, at this distance—
I will approach him nearer.

MANFRED (not perceiving the other). To be thus—
Gray—hair'd with anguish, like these blasted pines,
Wrecks of a single winter, barkless, branchless,
A blighted trunk upon a cursèd root
Which but supplies a feeling to decay—   330
And to be thus, eternally but thus,
Having been otherwise! Now furrowed o'er
With wrinkles, plough'd by moments, not by years
And hours—all tortured into ages—hours
Which I outlive!—Ye toppling crags of ice!
Ye avalanches, whom a breath draws down
In mountainous o'erwhelming, come and crush me!
I hear ye momently above, beneath,
Crash with a frequent conflict, but ye pass,
And only fall on things that still would live;   340
On the young flourishing forest, or the hut
And hamlet of the harmless villager.

CHAMOIS HUNTER. The mists begin to rise from up the valley;
I'll warn him to descend, or he may chance
To lose at once his way and life together.

MANFRED. The mists boil up around the glaciers; clouds
Rise curling fast beneath me, white and sulphury,
Like foam from the roused ocean of deep Hell,

Whose every wave breaks on a living shore
Heap'd with the damn'd like pebbles.—I am giddy.   350

CHAMOIS HUNTER. I must approach him cautiously; if near
A sudden step will startle him, and he
Seems tottering already.

MANFRED. Mountains have fallen,
Leaving a gap in the clouds, and with the shock
Rocking their Alpine brethren; filling up
The ripe green valleys with destruction's splinters;
Damming the rivers with a sudden dash,
Which crush'd the waters into mist, and made
Their fountains find another channel—thus,
Thus, in its old age, did Mount Rosenberg—   360
Why stood I not beneath it?

CHAMOIS HUNTER. Friend! have a care,
Your next step may be fatal!—for the love
Of him who made you, stand not on that brink!

MANFRED. (not hearing him). Such would have been for me a fitting tomb;
My bones had then been quiet in their depth;
They had not then been strewn upon the rocks
For the wind's pastime—as thus—thus they shall be—
In this one plunge.—Farewell, ye opening heavens!
Look not upon me thus reproachfully—
Ye were not meant for me—Earth! take these atoms!   370

[As MANFRED is in act to spring from the cliff, the CHAMOIS HUNTER seizes and retains him with a sudden grasp.

CHAMOIS HUNTER. Hold, madman!—though aweary of thy life,
Stain not our pure vales with thy guilty blood!

Away with me—I will not quit my hold.

MANFRED. I am most sick at heart—nay, grasp me not—
I am all feebleness—the mountains whirl
Spinning around me—I grow blind—What art thou?

CHAMOIS HUNTER. I'll answer that anon.—Away with me!
The clouds grow thicker—there—now lean on me—
Place your foot here—here, take this staff, and cling
A moment to that shrub—now give me your hand,   380
And hold fast by my girdle—softly—well—
The Chalet will be gain'd within an hour.
Come on, we'll quickly find a surer footing,
And something like a pathway, which the torrent
Hath wash'd since winter.—Come, 'tis bravely done;
You should have been a hunter.— Follow me.

[As they descend the rocks with difficulty, the scene closes.

ACT II
SCENE I

A Cottage amongst the Bernese Alps.

MANFRED and the CHAMOIS HUNTER.

CHAMOIS HUNTER. No, no, yet pause, thou must not yet go forth:
Thy mind and body are alike unfit
To trust each other, for some hours, at least;
When thou art better, I will be thy guide—
But whither?

MANFRED. It imports not; I do know
My route full well, and need no further guidance.

CHAMOIS HUNTER. Thy garb and gait bespeak thee of high lineage—
One of the many chiefs, whose castled crags
Look o'er the lower valleys—which of these
May call thee Lord? I only know their portals;   10
My way of life leads me but rarely down
To bask by the huge hearths of those old halls,
Carousing with the vassals, but the paths,
Which step from out our mountains to their doors,
I know from childhood—which of these is thine?

MANFRED. No matter.

CHAMOIS HUNTER. Well, sir, pardon me the question,
And be of better cheer. Come, taste my wine;
'Tis of an ancient vintage; many a day
'T has thaw'd my veins among our glaciers, now

Let it do thus for thine. Come, pledge me fairly.   20

MANFRED. Away, away! there's blood upon the brim!
Will it then never—never sink in the earth?

CHAMOIS HUNTER. What dost thou mean? thy senses wander from thee.

MANFRED. I say 't is blood—my blood! the pure warm stream
Which ran in the veins of my fathers, and in ours
When we were in our youth, and had one heart
And loved each other as we should not love,
And this was shed: but still it rises up
Colouring the clouds, that shut me out from heaven
Where thou art not—and I shall never be.   30

CHAMOIS HUNTER. Man of strange words, and some half-maddening sin
Which makes thee people vacancy, whate'er
Thy dread and sufferance be, there's comfort yet—
The aid of holy men, and heavenly patience—

MANFRED. Patience and patience! Hence—that word was made
For brutes of burthen, not for birds of prey;
Preach it to mortals of a dust like thine,—
I am not of thine order.

CHAMOIS HUNTER. Thanks to heaven!
I would not be of thine for the free fame
Of William Tell; but whatsoe'er thine ill,   40
It must be borne, and these wild starts are useless.

MANFRED. Do I not bear it?—Look on me—I live.

CHAMOIS HUNTER. This is convulsion, and no healthful life.

MANFRED. I tell thee, man! I have lived many years,
Many long years, but they are nothing now
To those which I must number: ages—ages—
Space and eternity—and consciousness,
With the fierce thirst of death—and still unslaked!

CHAMOIS HUNTER. Why, on thy brow the seal of middle age
Hath scarce been set; I am thine elder far.   50

MANFRED. Think'st thou existence doth depend on time?
It doth; but actions are our epochs: mine
Have made my days and nights imperishable
Endless, and all alike, as sands on the shore
Innumerable atoms; and one desert
Barren and cold, on which the wild waves break,
But nothing rests, save carcases and wrecks,
Rocks, and the salt-surf weeds of bitterness.

CHAMOIS HUNTER. Alas! he's mad—but yet I must not leave him.

MANFRED. I would I were—for then the things I see   60
Would be but a distemper'd dream.

CHAMOIS HUNTER. What is it
That thou dost see, or think thou look'st upon?

MANFRED. Myself, and thee—a peasant of the Alps—
Thy humble virtues, hospitable home
And spirit patient, pious, proud and free;
Thy self-respect, grafted on innocent thoughts;
Thy days of health, and nights of sleep; thy toils
By danger dignified, yet guiltless; hopes
Of cheerful old age and a quiet grave,
With cross and garland over its green turf,   70
And thy grandchildren's love for epitaph;

This do I see—and then I look within—
It matters not—my soul was scorch'd already!

CHAMOIS HUNTER. And would'st thou then exchange thy lot for mine?

MANFRED. No, friend! I would not wrong thee, nor exchange
My lot with living being: I can bear—
However wretchedly, 't is still to bear—
In life what others could not brook to dream,
But perish in their slumber.

CHAMOIS HUNTER.   And with this—
This cautious feeling for another's pain,   80
Canst thou be black with evil?—say not so.
Can one of gentle thoughts have wreak'd revenge
Upon his enemies?

MANFRED. Oh! no, no, no!
My injuries came down on those who loved me—
On those whom I best loved: I never quell'd
An enemy, save in my just defence—
But my embrace was fatal.

CHAMOIS HUNTER.   Heaven give thee rest!
And penitence restore thee to thyself;
My prayers shall be for thee.

MANFRED. I need them not,
But can endure thy pity. I depart—   90
'T is time—farewell!—Here's gold, and thanks for thee;
No words—it is thy due. Follow me not;
I know my path—the mountain peril's past:
And once again, I charge thee, follow not!   [Exit MANFRED.

SCENE II

A lower Valley in the Alps.—A Cataract.

Enter MANFRED.

It is not noon—the sunbow's rays still arch
The torrent with the many hues of heaven,
And roll the sheeted silver's waving column
O'er the crag's headlong perpendicular,
And fling its lines of foaming height along,
And to and fro, like the pale courser's tail,   100
The Giant steed, to be bestrode by Death,
As told in the Apocalypse. No eyes
But mine now drink this sight of loveliness;
I should be sole in this sweet solitude,
And with the Spirit of the place divide
The homage of these waters.—I will call her.

[MANFRED takes some of the water into the palm of his hand, and flings it in the air, muttering the adjuration. After a pause, the WITCH OF THE ALPS rises beneath the arch of the sunbow of the torrent.

Beautiful Spirit! with thy hair of light,
And dazzling eyes of glory, in whose form
The charms of Earth's least mortal daughters grow
To an unearthly stature, in an essence   110
Of purer elements; while the hues of youth
(Carnation'd like a sleeping infant's cheek
Rock'd by the beating of her mother's heart,
Or the rose tints, which summer's twilight leaves
Upon the lofty glacier's virgin snow,

The blush of earth embracing with her heaven)
Tinge thy celestial aspect, and make tame
The beauties of the sunbow which bends o'er thee.
Beautiful Spirit! in thy calm clear brow,
Wherein is glass'd serenity of soul,   120
Which of itself shows immortality,
I read that thou wilt pardon to a Son
Of Earth, whom the abstruser powers permit
At times to commune with them—if that he
Avail him of his spells—to call thee thus,
And gaze on thee a moment.

WITCH. Son of Earth!
I know thee, and the powers which give thee power;
I know thee for a man of many thoughts,
And deeds of good and ill, extreme in both,
Fatal and fated in thy sufferings.   130
I have expected this—what wouldst thou with me?

MANFRED. To look upon thy beauty—nothing further.
The face of the earth hath madden'd me, and I
Take refuge in her mysteries, and pierce
To the abodes of those who govern her—
But they can nothing aid me. I have sought
From them what they could not bestow, and now
I search no further.

WITCH. What could be the quest
Which is not in the power of the most powerful,
The rulers of the invisible?

MANFRED. A boon;   140
But why should I repeat it? 'twere in vain.

WITCH. I know not that; let thy lips utter it.

MANFRED. Well, though it torture me, 't is but the same;
My pang shall find a voice. From my youth upwards
My spirit walk'd not with the souls of men,
Nor look'd upon the earth with human eyes;
The thirst of their ambition was not mine;
The aim of their existence was not mine;
My joys, my griefs, my passions, and my powers,
Made me a stranger; though I wore the form,   150
I had no sympathy with breathing flesh,
Nor midst the creatures of clay that girded me
Was there but one who—but of her anon.
I said with men, and with the thoughts of men,
I held but slight communion; but instead,
My joy was in the Wilderness, to breathe
The difficult air of the iced mountain's top,
Where the birds dare not build, nor insect's wing
Flit o'er the herbless granite; or to plunge
Into the torrent, and to roll along   160
On the swift whirl of the new breaking wave
Of river-stream, or ocean, in their flow.
In these my early strength exulted; or
To follow through the night the moving moon,
The stars and their development, or catch
The dazzling lightnings till my eyes grew dim;
Or to look, list'ning, on the scatter'd leaves,
While Autumn winds were at their evening song.
These were my pastimes, and to be alone;
For if the beings, of whom I was one,—   170
Hating to be so,—cross'd me in my path,
I felt myself degraded back to them,
And was all clay again. And then I dived,
In my lone wanderings, to the caves of death,
Searching its cause in its effect, and drew
From wither'd bones, and skulls, and heap'd up dust,
Conclusions most forbidden. Then I pass'd

The nights of years in sciences, untaught
Save in the old-time; and with time and toil,
And terrible ordeal, and such penance   180
As in itself hath power upon the air
And spirits that do compass air and earth,
Space, and the peopled infinite, I made
Mine eyes familiar with Eternity,
Such as, before me, did the Magi, and
He who from out their fountain dwellings raised
Eros and Anteros, at Gadara,
As I do thee,—and with my knowledge grew
The thirst of knowledge, and the power and joy
Of this most bright intelligence, until—   190

WITCH. Proceed.

MANFRED. Oh! I but thus prolonged my words,
Boasting these idle attributes, because
As I approach the core of my heart's grief—
But to my task. I have not named to thee
Father or mother, mistress, friend, or being
With whom I wore the chain of human ties;
If I had such, they seem'd not such to me—
Yet there was one—

WITCH. Spare not thyself—proceed.

MANFRED. She was like me in lineaments—her eyes
Her hair, her features, all, to the very tone   200
Even of her voice, they said were like to mine;
But soften'd all, and temper'd into beauty;
She had the same lone thoughts and wanderings,
The quest of hidden knowledge, and a mind
To comprehend the universe: nor these
Alone, but with them gentler powers than mine,

Manfred

Pity, and smiles, and tears—which I had not;
And tenderness—but that I had for her;
Humility—and that I never had.
Her faults were mine—her virtues were her own— 210
I loved her, and destroy'd her!

WITCH. With thy hand?

MANFRED. Not with my hand, but heart—which broke her heart;
It gazed on mine, and wither'd. I have shed
Blood, but not hers—and yet her blood was shed—
I saw, and could not stanch it.

WITCH. And for this—
A being of the race thou dost despise,
The order which thine own would rise above,
Mingling with us and ours, thou dost forego
The gifts of our great knowledge, and shrink'st back
To recreant mortality—Away! 220

MANFRED. Daughter of Air! I tell thee, since that hour—
But words are breath—look on me in my sleep,
Or watch my watchings—Come and sit by me!
My solitude is solitude no more,
But peopled with the Furies,—I have gnash'd
My teeth in darkness till returning morn,
Then cursed myself till sunset;—I have pray'd
For madness as a blessing—'tis denied me.
I have affronted death—but in the war
Of elements the waters shrunk from me, 230
And fatal things pass'd harmless—the cold hand
Of an all-pitiless demon held me back,
Back by a single hair, which would not break.
In fantasy, imagination, all
The affluence of my soul—which one day was

A Croesus in creation—I plunged deep,
But, like an ebbing wave, it dash'd me back
Into the gulf of my unfathom'd thought.
I plunged amidst mankind—Forgetfulness
I sought in all, save where 'tis to be found,   240
And that I have to learn—my sciences,
My long pursued and superhuman art,
Is mortal here; I dwell in my despair—
And live—and live for ever.

WITCH. It may be
That I can aid thee.

MANFRED. To do this thy power
Must wake the dead, or lay me low with them.
Do so—in any shape—in any hour—
With any torture—so it be the last.

WITCH. That is not in my province; but if thou
Wilt swear obedience to my will, and do   250
My bidding, it may help thee to thy wishes.

MANFRED. I will not swear—Obey! and whom? the spirits
Whose presence I command, and be the slave
Of those who served me—Never!

WITCH. Is this all?
Hast thou no gentler answer?—Yet bethink thee,
And pause ere thou rejectest.

MANFRED. I have said it.

WITCH. Enough!—I may retire then—say!

MANFRED. Retire!   [The WITCH disappears.

Manfred

MANFRED (alone). We are the fools of time and terror: Days
Steal on us and steal from us; yet we live,
Loathing our life, and dreading still to die. 260
In all the days of this detested yoke—
This vital weight upon the struggling heart,
Which sinks with sorrow, or beats quick with pain,
Or joy that ends in agony or faintness—
In all the days of past and future, for
In life there is no present, we can number
How few, how less than few, wherein the soul
Forbears to pant for death, and yet draws back
As from a stream in winter, though the chill
Be but a moment's. I have one resource 270
Still in my science—I can call the dead,
And ask them what it is we dread to be:
The sternest answer can but be the Grave,
And that is nothing—if they answer not—
The buried Prophet answered to the Hag
Of Endor; and the Spartan Monarch drew
From the Byzantine maid's unsleeping spirit
An answer and his destiny—he slew
That which he loved unknowing what he slew,
And died unpardon'd—though he call'd in aid 280
The Phyxian Jove, and in Phigalia roused
The Arcadian Evocators to compel
The indignant shadow to depose her wrath,
Or fix her term of vengeance—she replied
In words of dubious import, but fulfill'd.
If I had never lived, that which I love
Had still been living; had I never loved,
That which I love would still be beautiful—
Happy and giving happiness. What is she?
What is she now?—a sufferer for my sins— 290
A thing I dare not think upon—or nothing.
Within few hours I shall not call in vain—

Yet in this hour I dread the thing I dare:
Until this hour I never shrunk to gaze
On spirit, good or evil—now I tremble,
And feel a strange cold thaw upon my heart.
But I can act even what I most abhor,
And champion human fears.—The night approaches. [Exit.

SCENE III

The Summit of the Jungfrau Mountain.

Enter FIRST DESTINY.

The moon is rising broad, and round, and bright;
And here on snows, where never human foot 300
Of common mortal trod, we nightly tread,
And leave no traces; o'er the savage sea,
The glassy ocean of the mountain ice,
We skim its rugged breakers, which put on
The aspect of a tumbling tempest's foam,
Frozen in a moment—a dead whirlpool's image.
And this most steep fantastic pinnacle,
The fretwork of some earthquake—where the clouds
Pause to repose themselves in passing by—
Is sacred to our revels, or our vigils; 310
Here do I wait my sisters, on our way
To the Hall of Arimanes, for to-night
Is our great festival—'t is strange they come not.

    A Voice without, singing.

   The Captive Usurper,
     Hurl'd down from the throne,
   Lay buried in torpor,
     Forgotten and lone;
   I broke through his slumbers,
     I shiver'd his chain,
   I leagued him with numbers— 320
     He's Tyrant again!
  With the blood of a million he'll answer my care,

With a nation's destruction—his flight and despair.

    Second Voice, without.

The ship sail'd on, the ship sail'd fast,
But I left not a sail, and I left not a mast;
There is not a plank of the hull or the deck,
And there is not a wretch to lament o'er his wreck;
Save one, whom I held, as he swam, by the hair,
And he was a subject well worthy my care;
A traitor on land, and a pirate at sea—   330
But I saved him to wreak further havoc for me!

    FIRST DESTINY, answering.

The city lies sleeping;
    The morn, to deplore it,
May dawn on it weeping:
    Sullenly, slowly,
The black plague flew o'er it—
    Thousands lie lowly;
Tens of thousands shall perish—
    The living shall fly from
The sick they should cherish;   340
    But nothing can vanquish
The touch that they die from.
    Sorrow and anguish,
And evil and dread,
    Envelope a nation—
The blest are the dead,
    Who see not the sight
Of their own desolation;
    This work of a night—
This wreck of a realm—this deed of my doing—   350
For ages I've done, and shall still be renewing!

Enter the SECOND and THIRD DESTINIES.

The Three.

> Our hands contain the hearts of men,
>   Our footsteps are their graves:
> We only give to take again
>   The spirits of our slaves!

FIRST DESTINY. Welcome!—Where's Nemesis?

SECOND DESTINY. At some great work;
But what I know not, for my hands were full.

THIRD DESTINY. Behold she cometh.

Enter NEMESIS.

FIRST DESTINY. Say, where hast thou been?
My sisters and thyself are slow to-night.

NEMESIS. I was detain'd repairing shattered thrones,   360
Marrying fools, restoring dynasties,
Avenging men upon their enemies,
And making them repent their own revenge;
Goading the wise to madness, from the dull
Shaping out oracles to rule the world
Afresh, for they were waxing out of date,
And mortals dared to ponder for themselves,
To weigh kings in the balance, and to speak
Of freedom, the forbidden fruit.—Away!
We have outstaid the hour—mount we our clouds! [Exeunt.   370

SCENE IV

The Hall of ARIMANES.—ARIMANES on his Throne, a Globe of Fire, surrounded by the SPIRITS.

    Hymn of the SPIRITS

  Hail to our Master!—Prince of Earth and Air!—
Who walks the clouds and waters—in his hand
The sceptre of the elements, which tear
   Themselves to chaos at his high command!
He breatheth—and a tempest shakes the sea;
   He speaketh—and the clouds reply in thunder;
He gazeth—from his glance the sunbeams flee;
   He moveth—earthquakes rend the world asunder.
Beneath his footsteps the volcanoes rise;
   His shadow is the Pestilence; his path   380
The comets herald through the crackling skies;
   And planets turn to ashes at his wrath.
To him War offers daily sacrifice;
   To him Death pays his tribute; Life is his,
With all its infinite of agonies—
   And his the spirit of whatever is!

    Enter the DESTINIES and NEMESIS.

FIRST DESTINY. Glory to Arimanes! on the earth
His power increaseth—both my sisters did
His bidding, nor did I neglect my duty!

SECOND DESTINY. Glory to Arimanes! we who bow   390
The necks of men, bow down before his throne!

THIRD DESTINY. Glory to Arimanes!—we await His nod!

NEMESIS. Sovereign of Sovereigns! we are thine.
And all that liveth, more or less, is ours,
And most things wholly so; still to increase
Our power, increasing thine, demands our care,
And we are vigilant—Thy late commands
Have been fulfill'd to the utmost.

   Enter MANFRED.

A SPIRIT. What is here?
A mortal!—Thou most rash and fatal wretch,
Bow down and worship!

SECOND SPIRIT. I do know the man—   400
A Magian of great power, and fearful skill!

THIRD SPIRIT. Bow down and worship, slave! What, know'st thou not
Thine and our Sovereign?—Tremble, and obey!

ALL THE SPIRITS. Prostrate thyself, and thy condemnèd clay,
Child of the Earth! or dread the worst.

MANFRED. I know it;
And yet ye see I kneel not.

FOURTH SPIRIT. 'T will be taught thee.

MANFRED. 'Tis taught already,—many a night on the earth,
On the bare ground, have I bow'd down my face,
And strew'd my head with ashes; I have known
The fulness of humiliation, for   410
I sunk before my vain despair, and knelt
To my own desolation.

FIFTH SPIRIT. Dost thou dare
Refuse to Arimanes on his throne
What the whole earth accords, beholding not
The terror of his Glory—Crouch! I say.

MANFRED. Bid him bow down to that which is above him,
The overruling Infinite—the Maker
Who made him not for worship—let him kneel,
And we will kneel together.

THE SPIRITS. Crush the worm!
Tear him in pieces!—

FIRST DESTINY. Hence! Avaunt!—he's mine.   420
Prince of the Powers invisible! This man
Is of no common order, as his port
And presence here denote. His sufferings
Have been of an immortal nature, like
Our own; his knowledge and his powers and will,
As far as is compatible with clay,
Which clogs the ethereal essence, have been such
As clay hath seldom borne; his aspirations
Have been beyond the dwellers of the earth,
And they have only taught him what we know—   430
That knowledge is not happiness, and science
But an exchange of ignorance for that
Which is another kind of ignorance.
This is not all; the passions, attributes
Of earth and heaven, from which no power, nor being,
Nor breath from the worm upwards is exempt,
Have pierced his heart; and in their consequence
Made him a thing, which I, who pity not,
Yet pardon those who pity. He is mine,
And thine, it may be—be it so, or not,   440
No other Spirit in this region hath

A soul like his—or power upon his soul.

NEMESIS. What doth he here then?

FIRST DESTINY. Let him answer that.

MANFRED. Ye know what I have known; and without power
I could not be amongst ye: but there are
Powers deeper still beyond—I come in quest
Of such, to answer unto what I seek.

NEMESIS. What wouldst thou?

MANFRED. Thou canst not reply to me.
Call up the dead—my question is for them.

NEMESIS. Great Arimanes, doth thy will avouch   450
The wishes of this mortal?

ARIMANES. Yea.

NEMESIS. Whom wouldst thou
Uncharnel?

MANFRED. One without a tomb—call up Astarte.

  NEMESIS

    Shadow! or Spirit!
      Whatever thou art,
    Which still doth inherit
      The whole or a part
    Of the form of thy birth,
      Of the mould of thy clay
    Which returned to the earth,—   460

> Re-appear to the day!
> Bear what thou borest,
>   The heart and the form,
> And the aspect thou worest
>   Redeem from the worm.
> Appear!—Appear!—Appear!
> Who sent thee there requires thee here!

[The Phantom of ASTARTE rises and stands in the midst.

MANFRED. Can this be death? there's bloom upon her cheek;
But now I see it is no living hue,
But a strange hectic—like the unnatural red   470
Which Autumn plants upon the perish'd leaf.
It is the same! Oh, God! that I should dread
To look upon the same—Astarte!—No,
I cannot speak to her—but bid her speak—
Forgive me or condemn me.

NEMESIS

> By the power which hath broken
>   The grave which enthrall'd thee,
> Speak to him who hath spoken,
>   Or those who have call'd thee!

MANFRED. She is silent,
And in that silence I am more than answer'd.   480

NEMESIS. My power extends no further.
Prince of air! It rests with thee alone—command her voice.

ARIMANES. Spirit—obey this sceptre!

NEMESIS.   Silent still!

She is not of our order, but belongs
To the other powers. Mortal! thy quest is vain,
And we are baffled also.

MANFRED. Hear me, hear me—
Astarte! my belovèd! speak to me;
I have so much endured—so much endure—
Look on me! the grave hath not changed thee more
Than I am changed for thee. Thou lovèdst me   490
Too much, as I loved thee: we were not made
To torture thus each other, though it were
The deadliest sin to love as we have loved.
Say that thou loath'st me not—that I do bear
This punishment for both—that thou wilt be
One of the blessèd—and that I shall die;
For hitherto all hateful things conspire
To bind me in existence—in a life
Which makes me shrink from immortality—
A future like the past. I cannot rest.   500
I know not what I ask, nor what I seek:
I feel but what thou art—and what I am;
And I would hear yet once before I perish
The voice which was my music—Speak to me!
For I have call'd on thee in the still night,
Startled the slumbering birds from the hush'd boughs,
And woke the mountain wolves, and made the caves
Acquainted with thy vainly echo'd name,
Which answer'd me—many things answer'd me—
Spirits and men—but thou wert silent all.   510
Yet speak to me! I have outwatch'd the stars,
And gazed o'er heaven in vain in search of thee.
Speak to me! I have wander'd o'er the earth,
And never found thy likeness—Speak to me!
Look on the fiends around—they feel for me:
I fear them not, and feel for thee alone.

Speak to me! though it be in wrath;—but say—
I reck not what—but let me hear thee once—
This once—once more!

PHANTOM OF ASTARTE. Manfred!

MANFRED. Say on, say on—
I live but in the sound—it is thy voice!   520

PHANTOM. Manfred! To-morrow ends thine earthly ills.
Farewell!

MANFRED.   Yet one word more—am I forgiven?

PHANTOM. Farewell!

MANFRED. Say, shall we meet again?

PHANTOM. Farewell!

MANFRED. One word for mercy! Say, thou lovest me.

PHANTOM. Manfred! [The Spirit of ASTARTE departs.

NEMESIS. She's gone, and will not be recall'd;
Her words will be fulfill'd. Return to the earth.

A SPIRIT. He is convulsed—This is to be a mortal
And seek the things beyond mortality.

ANOTHER SPIRIT. Yet, see, he mastereth himself, and makes
His torture tributary to his will.   530
Had he been one of us, he would have made
An awful spirit.

NEMESIS. Hast thou further question
Of our great sovereign, or his worshippers?
MANFRED. None.

NEMESIS. Then for a time farewell.

MANFRED. We meet then! Where? On the earth?—
Even as thou wilt: and for the grace accorded
I now depart a debtor. Fare ye well!   [Exit MANFRED.

   (Scene closes).

ACT III
SCENE I

A Hall in the Castle of Manfred.

MANFRED and HERMAN.

MANFRED. What is the hour?

HERMAN. It wants but one till sunset,
And promises a lovely twilight.

MANFRED. Say,
Are all things so disposed of in the tower
As I directed?

HERMAN. All, my lord, are ready;
Here is the key and casket.

MANFRED. It is well:
Thou mayst retire.   [Exit HERMAN.

MANFRED (alone).   There is a calm upon me—
Inexplicable stillness! which till now
Did not belong to what I knew of life.
If that I did not know philosophy
To be of all our vanities the motliest,   10
The merest word that ever fool'd the ear
From out the schoolman's jargon, I should deem
The golden secret, the sought 'Kalon,' found,
And seated in my soul. It will not last,
But it is well to have known it, though but once:
It hath enlarged my thoughts with a new sense,

And I within my tablets would note down
That there is such a feeling. Who is there?

    Re-enter HERMAN.

HERMAN. My lord, the abbot of St. Maurice craves
To greet your presence.

    Enter the ABBOT OF ST. MAURICE.

ABBOT. Peace be with Count Manfred!   20

MANFRED. Thanks, holy father! welcome to these walls;
Thy presence honours them, and blesseth those
Who dwell within them.

ABBOT. Would it were so, Count!—
But I would fain confer with thee alone.

MANFRED. Herman, retire.—What would my reverend guest?

ABBOT. Thus, without prelude:—Age and zeal, my office,
And good intent, must plead my privilege;
Our near, though not acquainted neighbourhood,
May also be my herald. Rumours strange,
And of unholy nature, are abroad,   30
And busy with thy name; a noble name
For centuries: may he who bears it now
Transmit it unimpair'd!

MANFRED. Proceed,—I listen.

ABBOT 'T is said thou holdest converse with the things
Which are forbidden to the search of man;
That with the dwellers of the dark abodes,

The many evil and unheavenly spirits
Which walk the valley of the shade of death,
Thou communest. I know that with mankind,
Thy fellows in creation, thou dost rarely   40
Exchange thy thoughts, and that thy solitude
Is as an anchorite's, were it but holy.

MANFRED. And what are they who do avouch these things?

ABBOT. My pious brethren, the scared peasantry,
Even thy own vassals, who do look on thee
With most unquiet eyes. Thy life's in peril.

MANFRED. Take it.

ABBOT. I come to save, and not destroy.
I would not pry into thy secret soul;
But if these things be sooth, there still is time
For penitence and pity: reconcile thee   50
With the true church, and through the church to heaven.

MANFRED. I hear thee. This is my reply, whate'er
I may have been, or am, doth rest between
Heaven and myself; I shall not choose a mortal
To be my mediator. Have I sinn'd
Against your ordinances? prove and punish!

ABBOT. My son! I did not speak of punishment,
But penitence and pardon; with thyself
The choice of such remains—and for the last,
Our institutions and our strong belief   60
Have given me power to smooth the path from sin
To higher hope and better thoughts, the first
I leave to heaven—'Vengeance is mine alone!'
So saith the Lord, and with all humbleness

His servant echoes back the awful word.

MANFRED. Old man! there is no power in holy men,
Nor charm in prayer, nor purifying form
Of penitence, nor outward look, nor fast,
Nor agony, nor, greater than all these,
The innate tortures of that deep despair   70
Which is remorse without the fear of hell
But all in all sufficient to itself
Would make a hell of heaven,—can exorcise
From out the unbounded spirit, the quick sense
Of its own sins, wrongs, sufferance, and revenge
Upon itself; there is no future pang
Can deal that justice on the self-condemn'd
He deals on his own soul.

ABBOT. All this is well;
For this will pass away, and be succeeded
By an auspicious hope, which shall look up   80
With calm assurance to that blessed place
Which all who seek may win, whatever be
Their earthly errors, so they be atoned:
And the commencement of atonement is
The sense of its necessity.—Say on—
And all our church can teach thee shall be taught;
And all we can absolve thee, shall be pardon'd.

MANFRED. When Rome's sixth Emperor was near his last,
The victim of a self-inflicted wound,
To shun the torments of a public death   90
From senates once his slaves, a certain soldier,
With show of loyal pity, would have staunch'd
The gushing throat with his officious robe;
The dying Roman thrust him back and said—
Some empire still in his expiring glance—

'It is too late—is this fidelity?'

ABBOT. And what of this?

MANFRED. I answer with the Roman—
'It is too late!'

ABBOT. It never can be so,
To reconcile thyself with thy own soul,
And thy own soul with heaven. Hast thou no hope? 100
'Tis strange—even those who do despair above,
Yet shape themselves some phantasy on earth,
To which frail twig they cling, like drowning men.

MANFRED. Ay—father! I have had those earthly visions
And noble aspirations in my youth,
To make my own the mind of other men,
The enlightener of nations; and to rise
I knew not whither—it might be to fall;
But fall, even as the mountain—cataract,
Which having leapt from its more dazzling height, 110
Even in the foaming strength of its abyss
(Which casts up misty columns that become
Clouds raining from the re-ascended skies)
Lies low but mighty still.—But this is past,
My thoughts mistook themselves.

ABBOT. And wherefore so?

MANFRED. I could not tame my nature down; for he
Must serve who fain would sway—and soothe, and sue,
And watch all time, and pry into all place,
And be a living lie, who would become
A mighty thing amongst the mean, and such 120
The mass are; I disdain'd to mingle with

Manfred

A herd, though to be leader—and of wolves.
The lion is alone, and so am I.

ABBOT. And why not live and act with other men?

MANFRED. Because my nature was averse from life;
And yet not cruel; for I would not make,
But find a desolation. Like the wind,
The red—hot breath of the most lone Simoom,
Which dwells but in the desert, and sweeps o'er
The barren sands which bear no shrubs to blast   130
And revels o'er their wild and arid waves,
And seeketh not, so that it is not sought,
But being met is deadly,—such hath been
The course of my existence; but there came
Things in my path which are no more.

ABBOT. Alas!
I 'gin to fear that thou art past all aid
From me and from my calling; yet so young,
I still would—

MANFRED. Look on me! there is an order
Of mortals on the earth, who do become
Old in their youth, and die ere middle age,   140
Without the violence of warlike death;
Some perishing of pleasure, some of study,
Some worn with toil, some of mere weariness,
Some of disease, and some insanity,
And some of wither'd or of broken hearts;
For this last is a malady which slays
More than are number'd in the lists of Fate,
Taking all shapes, and bearing many names.
Look upon me! for even of all these things
Have I partaken; and of all these things,   150

One were enough; then wonder not that I
Am what I am, but that I ever was,
Or, having been, that I am still on earth.

ABBOT. Yet, hear me still—

MANFRED. Old man! I do respect
Thine order, and revere thine years; I deem
Thy purpose pious, but it is in vain.
Think me not churlish; I would spare thyself,
Far more than me, in shunning at this time
All further colloquy; and so—farewell.   [Exit MANFRED.

ABBOT. This should have been a noble creature: he   160
Hath all the energy which would have made
A goodly frame of glorious elements,
Had they been wisely mingled; as it is,
It is an awful chaos—light and darkness,
And mind and dust—and passions and pure thoughts,
Mix'd, and contending without end or order,
All dormant or destructive. He will perish,
And yet he must not; I will try once more,
For such are worth redemption; and my duty
Is to dare all things for a righteous end.   170
I'll follow him—but cautiously, though surely. [Exit ABBOT.

SCENE II

Another Chamber.

MANFRED and HERMAN.

HERMAN. My Lord, you bade me wait on you at sunset:
He sinks beyond the mountain.

MANFRED. Doth he so?
I will look on him.

[MANFRED advances to the Window of the Hall.

Glorious Orb! the idol
Of early nature, and the vigorous race
Of undiseased mankind the giant sons
Of the embrace of angels, with a sex
More beautiful than they, which did draw down
The erring spirits who can ne'er return;
Most glorious orb! that wert a worship, ere   180
The mystery of thy making was reveal'd!
Thou earliest minister of the Almighty,
Which gladden'd, on their mountain tops, the hearts
Of the Chaldean shepherds, till they pour'd
Themselves in orisons! Thou material God!
And representative of the Unknown,
Who chose thee for his shadow! Thou chief star!
Centre of many stars! which mak'st our earth
Endurable, and temperest the hues
And hearts of all who walk within thy rays!   190
Sire of the seasons! Monarch of the climes
And those who dwell in them! for near or far

Our inborn spirits have a tint of thee,
Even as our outward aspects;—thou dost rise,
And shine, and set in glory. Fare thee well!
I ne'er shall see thee more. As my first glance
Of love and wonder was for thee, then take
My latest look: thou wilt not beam on one
To whom the gifts of life and warmth have been
Of a more fatal nature. He is gone;   200
I follow.   [Exit MANFRED.

SCENE III

The Mountains.—The Castle of MANFRED at some distance.—A Terrace before a Tower.—Time, Twilight.

HERMAN, MANUEL, and other Dependants of MANFRED.

HERMAN. 'T is strange enough; night after night, for years,
He hath pursued long vigils in this tower,
Without a witness. I have been within it,—
So have we all been oft-times; but from it
Or its contents, it were impossible
To draw conclusions absolute of aught
His studies tend to. To be sure, there is
One chamber where none enter: I would give
The fee of what I have to come these three years   210
To pore upon its mysteries.

MANUEL. 'T were dangerous;
Content thyself with what thou know'st already.

HERMAN. Ah! Manuel! thou art elderly and wise,
And could'st say much; thou hast dwelt within the castle—
How many years is't?

MANUEL. Ere Count Manfred's birth,
I served his father, whom he nought resembles.

HERMAN. There be more sons in like predicament.
But wherein do they differ?

MANUEL. I speak not
Of features or of form, but mind and habits;
Count Sigismund was proud, but gay and free—   220
A warrior and a reveller; he dwelt not
With books and solitude, nor made the night
A gloomy vigil, but a festal time,
Merrier than day; he did not walk the rocks
And forests like a wolf, nor turn aside
From men and their delights.

HERMAN. Beshrew the hour,
But those were jocund times! I would that such
Would visit the old walls again; they look
As if they had forgotten them.

MANUEL. These walls
Must change their chieftain first. Oh! I have seen   230
Some strange things in them, Herman.

HERMAN. Come, be friendly;
Relate me some to while away our watch:
I've heard thee darkly speak of an event
Which happen'd hereabouts, by this same tower.

MANUEL. That was a night indeed! I do remember

'T was twilight, as it may be now, and such
Another evening; yon red cloud, which rests
On Eigher's pinnacle, so rested then,—
So like that it might be the same; the wind
Was faint and gusty, and the mountain snows   240
Began to glitter with the climbing moon.
Count Manfred was, as now, within his tower,—
How occupied, we knew not, but with him
The sole companion of his wanderings
And watchings—her, whom of all earthly things
That lived, the only thing he seem'd to love,—
As he, indeed, by blood was bound to do,
The Lady Astarte, his—
 Hush! who comes here?

    Enter the ABBOT.

ABBOT. Where is your master?

HERMAN. Yonder in the tower.

ABBOT. I must speak with him.

MANUEL. 'T is impossible;   250
He is most private, and must not be thus
Intruded on.

ABBOT.   Upon myself I take
The forfeit of my fault, if fault there be—
But I must see him.

HERMAN. Thou hast seen him once
This eve already.

ABBOT. Herman! I command thee,

Knock, and apprize the Count of my approach.

HERMAN. We dare not.

ABBOT. Then it seems I must be herald
Of my own purpose.

MANUEL. Reverend father, stop—
I pray you pause.

ABBOT. Why so?

MANUEL. But step this way,
And I will tell you further.   [Exeunt.   260

SCENE IV

Interior of the Tower.

MANFRED alone.

The stars are forth, the moon above the tops
Of the snow-shining mountains.—Beautiful!
I linger yet with Nature, for the night
Hath been to me a more familiar face
Than that of man; and in her starry shade
Of dim, and solitary loveliness,
I learn'd the language of another world.
I do remember me, that in my youth,
When I was wandering,—upon such a night
I stood within the Coloseum's wall,   270
Midst the chief relics of almighty Rome.
The trees which grew along the broken arches
Waved dark in the blue midnight, and the stars
Shone through the rents of ruin; from afar
The watchdog bay'd beyond the Tiber; and
More near from out the Caesars' palace came
The owl's long cry, and, interruptedly,
Of distant sentinels the fitful song
Begun and died upon the gentle wind.
Some cypresses beyond the time—worn breach 280
Appear'd to skirt the horizon, yet they stood
Within a bowshot. Where the Caesars dwelt,
And dwell the tuneless birds of night, amidst
A grove which springs through levell'd battlements,
And twines its roots with the imperial hearths,
Ivy usurps the laurel's place of growth;—
But the gladiators' bloody Circus stands,

A noble wreck in ruinous perfection!
While Caesar's chambers, and the Augustan halls
Grovel on earth in indistinct decay.— 290
And thou didst shine, thou rolling moon, upon
All this, and cast a wide and tender light,
Which soften'd down the hoar austerity
Of rugged desolation, and fill'd up,
As 'twere anew, the gaps of centuries;
Leaving that beautiful which still was so,
And making that which was not, till the place
Became religion, and the heart ran o'er
With silent worship of the great of old,—
The dead, but sceptred sovereigns, who still rule 300
Our spirits from their urns.—
'T was such a night!
'T is strange that I recall it at this time;
But I have found our thoughts take wildest flight
Even at the moment when they should array
Themselves in pensive order.

        Enter the ABBOT.

ABBOT. My good Lord!
I crave a second grace for this approach;
But yet let not my humble zeal offend
By its abruptness—all it hath of ill
Recoils on me; its good in the effect
May light upon your head—could I say heart— 310
Could I touch that, with words or prayers, I should
Recall a noble spirit which hath wander'd
But is not yet all lost.

MANFRED. Thou know'st me not;
My days are number'd, and my deeds recorded:
Retire, or 't will be dangerous—Away!

ABBOT. Thou dost not mean to menace me?

MANFRED. Not I;
I simply tell thee peril is at hand,
And would preserve thee.

ABBOT. What dost thou mean?

MANFRED. Look there!
What dost thou see?

ABBOT. Nothing.

MANFRED. Look there, I say,
And steadfastly;—now tell me what thou seest?   320

ABBOT. That which should shake me—but I fear it not;
I see a dusk and awful figure rise,
Like an infernal god from out the earth;
His face wrapt in a mantle, and his form
Robed as with angry clouds: he stands between
Thyself and me—but I do fear him not.

MANFRED. Thou hast no cause; he shall not harm thee, but
His sight may shock thine old limbs into palsy.
I say to thee—Retire!

ABBOT. And, I reply,
Never—till I have battled with this fiend:—   330
What doth he here?

MANFRED. Why—ay—what doth he here?
I did not send for him,—he is unbidden.

ABBOT. Alas! lost mortal! what with guests like these

Hast thou to do? I tremble for thy sake:
Why doth he gaze on thee, and thou on him?
Ah! he unveils his aspect; on his brow
The thunder-scars are graven; from his eye
Glares forth the immortality of hell—
Avaunt!—

MANFRED. Pronounce—what is thy mission?

SPIRIT. Come!

ABBOT. What art thou, unknown being? answer!—speak! 340

SPIRIT. The genius of this mortal.—Come! 't is time.

MANFRED. I am prepared for all things, but deny
The power which summons me. Who sent thee here?

SPIRIT. Thou'lt know anon—Come! Come!

MANFRED. I have commanded
Things of an essence greater far than thine,
And striven with thy masters. Get thee hence!

SPIRIT. Mortal! thine hour is come—Away! I say.

MANFRED. I knew, and know my hour is come, but not
To render up my soul to such as thee:
Away! I'll die as I have lived—alone. 350

SPIRIT. Then I must summon up my brethren.—Rise!
　　　　　　[Other spirits rise up.

ABBOT. Avaunt! ye evil ones!—Avaunt! I say,—
Ye have no power where piety hath power,

And I do charge ye in the name—

SPIRIT. Old man!
We know ourselves, our mission, and thine order;
Waste not thy holy words on idle uses,
It were in vain; this man is forfeited.
Once more I summon him—Away! away!

MANFRED. I do defy ye,—though I feel my soul
Is ebbing from me, yet I do defy ye;   360
Nor will I hence, while I have earthly breath
To breathe my scorn upon ye—earthly strength
To wrestle, though with spirits; what ye take
Shall be ta'en limb by limb.

SPIRIT. Reluctant mortal!
Is this the Magian who would so pervade
The world invisible, and make himself
Almost our equal?—Can it be that thou
Art thus in love with life? the very life
Which made thee wretched!

MANFRED. Thou false fiend, thou liest!
My life is in its last hour,—that I know,   370
Nor would redeem a moment of that hour.
I do not combat against death, but thee
And thy surrounding angels; my past power
Was purchased by no compact with thy crew,
But by superior science—penance—daring,
And length of watching—strength of mind—and skill
In knowledge of our fathers when the earth
Saw men and spirits walking side by side
And gave ye no supremacy: I stand
Upon my strength—I do defy—deny—   380
Spurn back, and scorn ye!—

Manfred

SPIRIT. But thy many crimes
Have made thee—

MANFRED.   What are they to such as thee?
Must crimes be punish'd but by other crimes,
And greater criminals?—Back to thy hell!
Thou hast no power upon me, that I feel;
Thou never shalt possess me, that I know:
What I have done is done; I bear within
A torture which could nothing gain from thine.
The mind which is immortal makes itself
Requital for its good or evil thoughts,   390
Is its own origin of ill and end,
And its own place and time; its innate sense,
When stripp'd of this mortality, derives
No colour from the fleeting things without,
But is absorb'd in sufferance or in joy,
Born from the knowledge of its own desert.
Thou didst not tempt me, and thou couldst not tempt me;
I have not been thy dupe nor am thy prey,
But was my own destroyer, and will be
My own hereafter.—Back, ye baffled fiends!   400
The hand of death is on me—but not yours!
            [The Demons disappear.

ABBOT. Alas! how pale thou art—thy lips are white—
And thy breast heaves—and in thy gasping throat
The accents rattle. Give thy prayers to Heaven—
Pray—albeit but in thought,—but die not thus.

MANFRED. 'T is over—my dull eyes can fix thee not;
But all things swim around me, and the earth
Heaves as it were beneath me. Fare thee well—
Give me thy hand.

ABBOT. Cold—cold—even to the heart—
But yet one prayer—Alas! how fares it with thee?   410

MANFRED. Old man! 't is not so difficult to die.   [MANFRED expires.

ABBOT. He's gone, his soul hath ta'en its earthless flight;
Whither? I dread to think; but he is gone.

www.ingramcontent.com/pod-product-compliance
Lightning Source LLC
Chambersburg PA
CBHW031427040426
42444CB00006B/726